Macmillan/McGraw-Hill **TIMELINKS**

All Together

PROGRAM AUTHORS
James A. Banks
Kevin P. Colleary
Linda Greenow
Walter C. Parker
Emily M. Schell
Dinah Zike

CONTRIBUTORS
Raymond C. Jones
Irma M. Olmedo

 Macmillan/McGraw-Hill

Geography

PROGRAM AUTHORS

James A. Banks, Ph.D.
Kerry and Linda Killinger Professor
  of Diversity Studies and Director, Center
  for Multicultural Education
University of Washington
Seattle, Washington

Kevin P. Colleary, Ed.D.
Curriculum and Teaching Department
Graduate School of Education
Fordham University
New York, New York

Linda Greenow, Ph.D.
Associate Professor and Chair
Department of Geography
State University of New York at New Paltz
New Paltz, New York

Walter C. Parker, Ph.D.
Professor of Social Studies Education,
  Adjunct Professor of Political Science
University of Washington
Seattle, Washington

Emily M. Schell, Ed.D.
Visiting Professor, Teacher Education
San Diego State University
San Diego, California

Dinah Zike
Educational Consultant
Dinah-Mite Activities, Inc.
San Antonio, Texas

CONTRIBUTORS

Raymond C. Jones, Ph.D.
Director of Secondary Social Studies
  Education
Wake Forest University
Winston-Salem, North Carolina

Irma M. Olmedo
Associate Professor
University of Illinois-Chicago
College of Education
Chicago, Illinois

HISTORIANS/SCHOLARS

Brooks Green, Ph.D.
Associate Professor of Geography
University of Central Arkansas
Conway, Arkansas

GRADE LEVEL REVIEWERS

Robin Bastolla
First Grade Teacher
Warnsdorfer School
East Brunswick, New Jersey

Kathleen Rose
First Grade Teacher
Bellerive Elementary School
St. Louis, Missouri

Amy Zewicki
First Grade Teacher
Jefferson Elementary School
Appleton, Wisconsin

EDITORIAL ADVISORY BOARD

Bradley R. Bakle
Assistant Superintendent
East Allen County Schools
New Haven, Indiana

Marilyn Barr
Assistant Superintendent for Instruction
Clyde-Savannah Central School
Clyde, New York

Lisa Bogle
Elementary Coordinator, K-5
Rutherford County Schools
Murfreesboro, Tennessee

Janice Buselt
Campus Support, Primary and ESOL
Wichita Public Schools
Wichita, Kansas

Kathy Cassioppi
Social Studies Coordinator
Rockford Public Schools, District 205
Rockford, Illinois

Denise Johnson, Ph.D.
Social Studies Supervisor
Knox County Schools
Knoxville, Tennessee

Steven Klein, Ph.D.
Social Studies Coordinator
Illinois School District U-46
Elgin, Illinois

Sondra Markman
Curriculum Director
Warren Township Board of Education
Warren Township, New Jersey

Cathy Nelson
Social Studies Coordinator
Columbus Public Schools
Columbus, Ohio

Holly Pies
Social Studies Coordinator
Vigo County Schools
Terre Haute, Indiana

Avon Ruffin
Social Studies County Supervisor
Winston-Salem/Forsyth Schools
Lewisville, North Carolina

Chuck Schierloh
Social Studies Curriculum Team Leader
Lima City Schools
Lima, Ohio

Bob Shamy
Social Studies Supervisor
East Brunswick Public Schools
East Brunswick, New Jersey

Judy Trujillo
Social Studies Coordinator
Columbia Missouri School District
Columbia, Missouri

Gayle Voyles
Director of the Center for Economic
  Education
Kansas City School District
Kansas City, Missouri

Todd Wigginton
Coordinator of Social Studies K-12
Metropolitan Nashville Public Schools
Nashville, Tennessee

 Students with print disabilities may be eligible to obtain an accessible, audio version of the pupil edition of this textbook. Please call Recording for the Blind & Dyslexic at 1-800-221-4792 for complete information.
learning through listening

The McGraw·Hill Companies

 **Macmillan McGraw-Hill**

MHID 0-02-152396-7   ISBN 978-0-02-152396-2   Printed in the United States of America

5 6 7 8 9 10 QVR/LEH 13 12

All Together

Table of Contents

Unit 2 All About Earth

 How do we learn about where we live?

Skills and Features

Maps

Unit 2

How do we learn about where we live?

Find out more about where we live at
www.macmillanmh.com

All About Earth

People, Places, and Events

Sarah

Sarah and her family live in Alaska.

For more about People, Places, and Events, visit
www.macmillanmh.com

Barrow, Alaska

In **Barrow, Alaska** it stays dark outside from November to January.

Dog Sledding

Sarah and her family enjoy **dog sledding** over the frozen land.

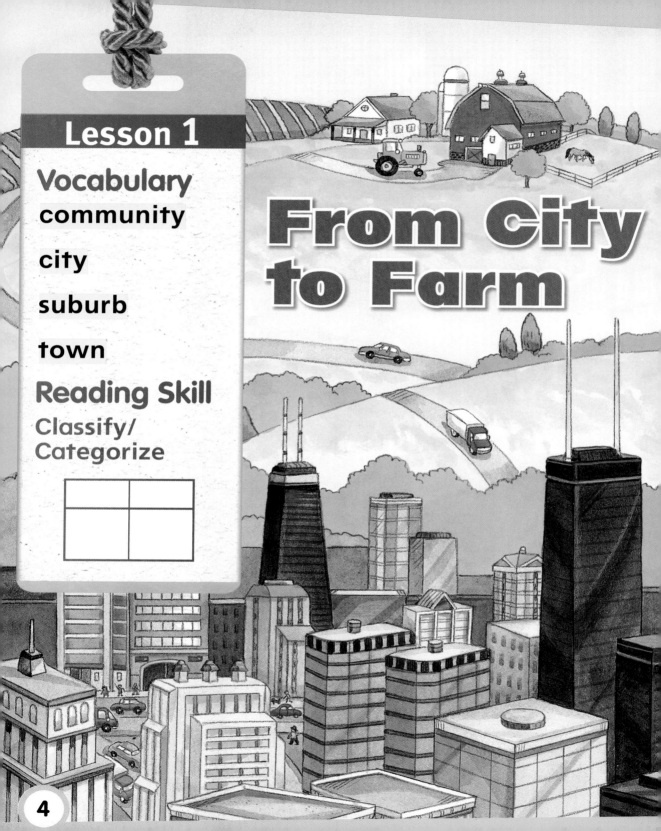

Lesson 1

Vocabulary

community

city

suburb

town

Reading Skill

Classify/
Categorize

From City to Farm

A City

A **community** is a place where people live, work, and have fun together. Welcome to the **city** of Chicago! A city is a big and busy community where many people work and live.

In a city you might live in a tall building. You could look down and see people and cars on the street below.

 What is special about a city?

Chicago

Suburbs and Towns

Chicago

Brookfield

Welcome to Brookfield, a **suburb** of Chicago. A suburb is a community located near a city.

In Brookfield, you might live in a house. You could play in your backyard with your friends. You might also play in a big park.

Many people live in Brookfield but work in Chicago. They might take a bus, train, or car to work every day.

 Where is a suburb located?

Places
Lakewood, Ohio

Lakewood is a suburb near Cleveland. If you lived in Lakewood, you could ride a bus, train, or car to visit the Children's Museum in Cleveland.

Towns and Farms

Manteno is a **town** in Illinois. A town is much smaller than a city. It is smaller than most suburbs, too. Farms are located near towns like Manteno.

If you lived on a farm, you could have lots of open space. Your family might grow food, like corn or tomatoes. You might help feed the cows and horses.

On days off from school, you could go to the nearest town with your family. You could shop or see a movie.

 What is it like to live on a farm?

Check Understanding

1. **Vocabulary** What is a **city**?

2. **Classify/Categorize** What things might you see in a city? On a farm?

3. Why do you think it is noisier in a city than in a town?

Lesson 2

Vocabulary

transportation

diagram

Reading Skill

Classify/
Categorize

People Change the Land

Changing the Land

Homes are built every day. Often, workers have to cut down trees and smooth out the land.

Sometimes builders have to change the way the water flows! It takes a lot of work to make a community.

How do workers build homes?

Moving from Place to Place

The way people move from place to place is called **transportation**. People drive cars, trucks, and buses on the roads and over bridges. They ride trains over the train tracks. They fly across the sky in airplanes, too!

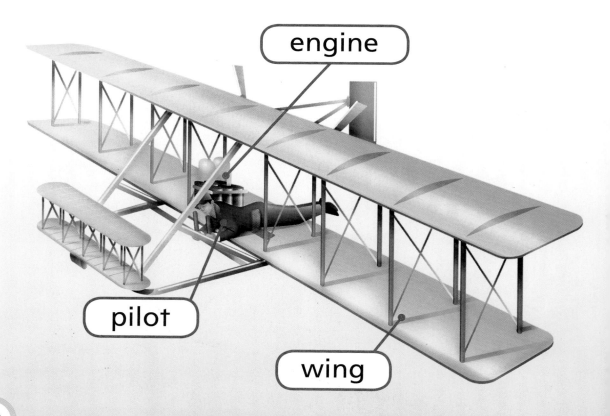

engine

pilot

wing

Look at the **diagram** on page 12.
A diagram shows the parts of
something. This diagram shows the
first airplane. It was built by the
Wright brothers over 100 years ago.

 What is transportation?

Check Understanding

1. **Vocabulary** What does a **diagram**
   show?

2. **Classify/Categorize**
   How do people travel?

3. **EXPLORE The Big Idea** Why do people make roads,
   bridges, and train tracks?

Looking at Earth

Lesson 3

Vocabulary

Earth

mountain

plain

hill

ocean

river

lake

Reading Skill

Classify/
Categorize

Land and Water

We live in different communities. We live in cities, suburbs, towns, and farms. But we all live together on **Earth**.

Earth is our home. Earth is made up of land and water.

What is Earth made of?

land

water

mountain

Different Kinds of Land

A **mountain** is the highest kind of land on Earth. Take a hike with your family in the Black Mountains of North Carolina!

A **plain** is a large, flat area of land. Go for a run across the plains of South Dakota. Watch out for the bison!

plain

hill

A **hill** is smaller than a mountain, but higher than a plain. Look at the beautiful flowers as you hike across the hills of Washington.

 What are plains?

Around the World

Rita lives in Italy near the Alps. The Alps are mountains. Italy also has hills and plains.

Water All Around

There is more water than land on Earth. The largest body of water is called an **ocean**. Take a swim in the Atlantic Ocean on a New Jersey beach.

A **river** is a long stream of water that flows into a larger body of water. Ride a raft on the Colorado River in Arizona.

river

ocean

A **lake** is a body of water with land all around it. Catch a walleye fish in Swamp Lake in Minnesota.

lake

 What is a river?

Check Understanding

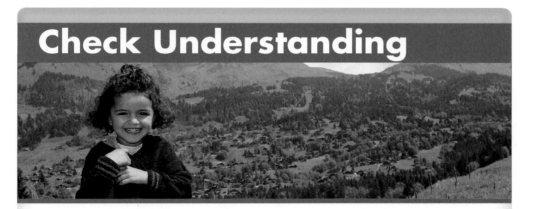

1. **Vocabulary** What is an **ocean**?

2. **Classify/Categorize** What kinds of land and water can you name?

3. What kinds of land and water are near your home?

Use Globes and Maps

Vocabulary

globe

map

Look at this **globe**. It is a model of Earth. You can spin a globe to see every part of Earth. Earth is round.

A **map** is a drawing of a place. Look at the map on the next page. This map shows all of Earth on one flat paper.

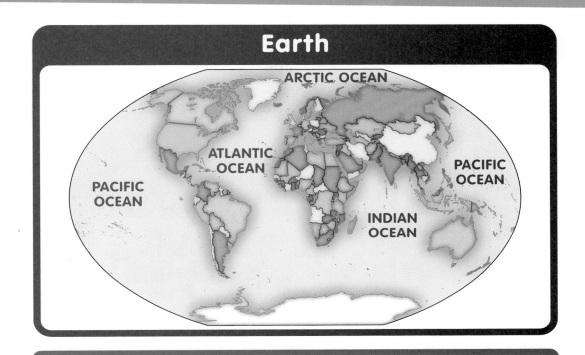

Earth

ARCTIC OCEAN

ATLANTIC OCEAN

PACIFIC OCEAN

PACIFIC OCEAN

INDIAN OCEAN

Try the Skill

1. What is a **globe**?

2. How is a map different from a globe?

Writing Activity Find an ocean on a globe. Write its name. Now find the same ocean on a map.

Learning about Earth

Lesson 4

Vocabulary

weather

season

natural resource

recycle

Reading Skill

Classify/ Categorize

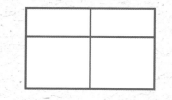

Weather

What did you wear to school today? Does your answer have something to do with **weather**? Weather is how hot, cold, wet, or dry it is outside.

At Sarah's house in Alaska, it is snowing. At the same time, it might be sunny at your house!

 What is weather?

summer

fall

Seasons

In some places, the weather changes with the **seasons**. A season is one of the four parts of the year. The four seasons are summer, fall, winter, and spring.

In the summer it is hot in many places. Leaves drop from trees in the fall. In the winter it can be snowy and cold. In the spring, new plants grow.

winter

spring

 Can you name the four seasons?

Event
Bears Hibernate in Winter

When it is cold, bears go into a deep sleep inside a cozy den. They sleep for most of the winter!

air

water

soil

sun

Caring About Earth

Air, water, soil, and the sun are all natural resources. A **natural resource** is something in nature that we use.

We take care of natural resources when we **recycle**. Recycle means to change a thing into something new and useful.

We can recycle our newspapers into new paper. We can use our bottles and jars again and again.

We can use less water, too. If we use less water now, we will still have water years from now.

 How can you take care of natural resources?

Check Understanding

1. **Vocabulary** What are **natural resources**?

2. **Classify/Categorize** What kinds of things can you do in winter? In summer?

3. How do the seasons change where you live?

Citizenship

Democracy in Action

Respecting Earth

To respect means to treat as important. We show respect for Earth by keeping it clean.

Please stop! Do not make someone else pick up your trash!

Joe saw Emily dropping her trash.
He helped Emily respect Earth.
What would you do?

Our World

Vocabulary

state

country

continent

Reading Skill

Classify/
Categorize

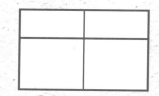

Our State and Our Country

A **state** is one part of a country.
A **country** is a land and the people who live there.

Our country is called the United States of America. We have 50 states in our country.

 How many states are in our country?

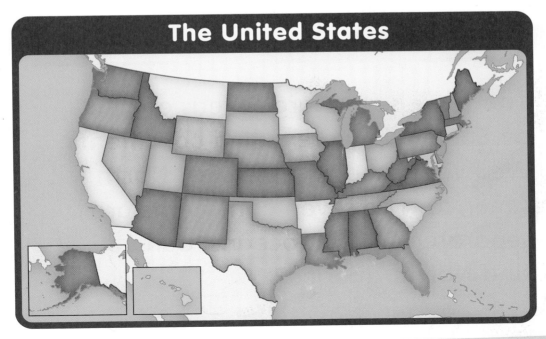

The United States

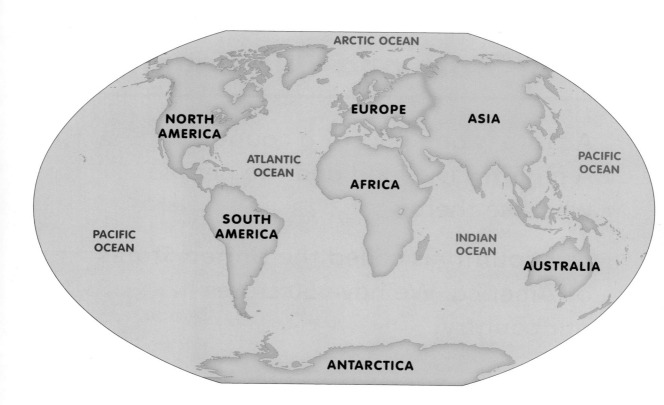

Our Continent

There are seven large areas of land on Earth. They are called **continents**. We live on the continent of North America. The seven continents are separated by four oceans. Can you find North America?

Can you name the four oceans?

People

Ellen Ochoa, Astronaut

Ellen was the first Hispanic American woman to fly in the space shuttle. She said, "I never got tired of watching the Earth . . . as we passed over it."

state

home

neighborhood

Where You Live

You belong to many places. There are many ways to name the places where you live.

 Where in the world do you live?

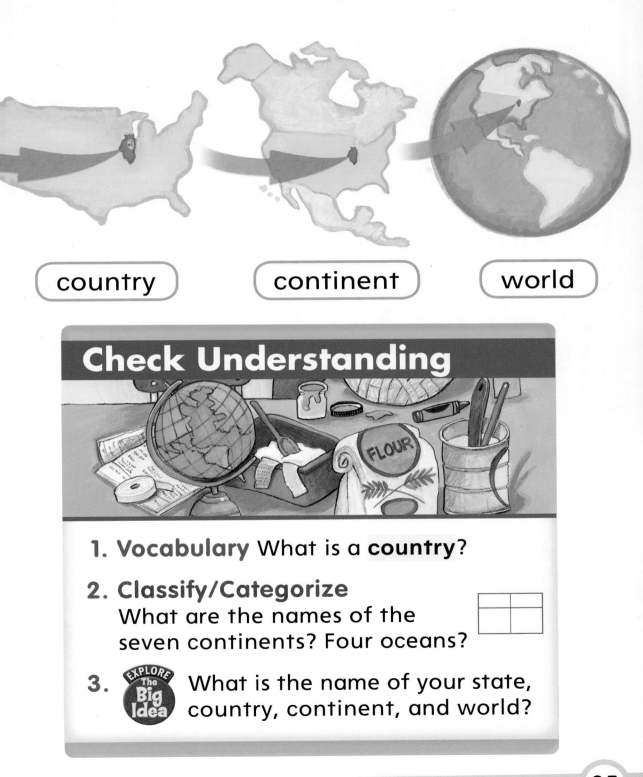

country   continent   world

Check Understanding

1. **Vocabulary** What is a **country**?

2. **Classify/Categorize**
   What are the names of the
   seven continents? Four oceans?

3. **EXPLORE The Big Idea** What is the name of your state,
   country, continent, and world?

Vocabulary

Number a paper from 1 to 3. Next to each number write the word that matches the meaning.

suburb   **mountain**   **lake**

1. an area located near a city

2. a body of water with land all around it

3. the highest kind of land

Critical Thinking

4. What are some ways that you use water?

5. Why do people change the land?

Skill

Use Globes and Maps

Look at the map of Earth. Answer the question below.

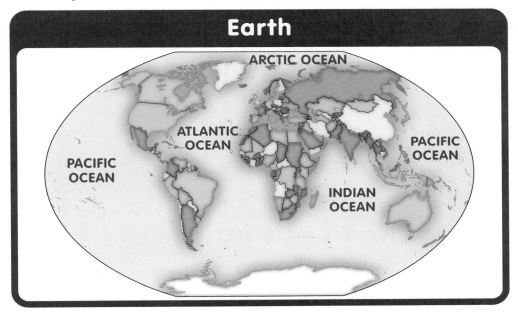

Earth

ARCTIC OCEAN

ATLANTIC OCEAN

PACIFIC OCEAN

PACIFIC OCEAN

INDIAN OCEAN

6. What parts of Earth are blue on the globe and on the map?

A. continents

B. oceans

C. countries

The Big Idea Geography Activity

Color a World Map

1 Color the oceans blue on a world map.

2 Trace each of the seven continents in a different color. You can use any colors, except blue.

3 Find North America on the world map. Draw a house to show where you live.

Picture Glossary

C

city A **city** is a big and busy place where many people work and live. (page 5)

community A **community** is a place where people live, work, and have fun together. (page 5)

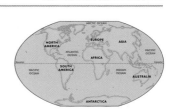

continent A **continent** is one of the seven large areas of land on Earth. (page 32)

country A **country** is a land and the people who live there. (page 31)

D

diagram A **diagram** is a picture that shows the parts of something. (page 13)

E

Earth **Earth** is our home. It is made of land and water. (page 15)

G

globe A **globe** is a model of Earth. (page 20)

H

hill A **hill** is smaller than a mountain, but higher than a plain. (page 17)

L

lake A **lake** is a body of water with land all around it. (page 19)

M

map A **map** is a drawing of a place. (page 20)

mountain A **mountain** is the highest kind of land. (page 16)

N

natural resource A **natural resource** is something in nature that we use. (page 26)

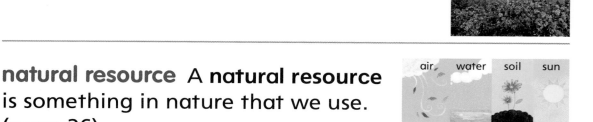

air   water   soil   sun

O ──────────────────────────────

ocean An **ocean** is the largest body of water. (page 18)

P ──────────────────────────────

plain A **plain** is a large, flat area of land. (page 16)

R ──────────────────────────────

recycle **Recycle** means to change a thing into something new and useful. (page 26)

river A **river** is a long stream of water that flows into a larger body of water. (page 18)

S ──────────────────────────────

season A **season** is one of the four parts of the year. They are summer, fall, winter, and spring. (page 24)

state A **state** is one part of a country. (page 31)

suburb A **suburb** is a place located near a city. (page 6)

town A **town** is a place where people live and work. It is smaller than a city. (page 8)

transportation **Transportation** is the way people move from place to place. (page 12)

weather **Weather** is how hot, cold, wet, or dry it is outside. (page 23)

Index

This index lists many things you can find in your book. It tells the page numbers on which they are found. If you see the letter *m* before a page number, you will find a map on that page.

Index

Credits

Maps: XNR

Illustrations: 4: Linda Howard Bittner. 6-7 Linda Howard Bittner. 8: Linda Howard Bittner. 9: Linda Howard Bittner. 12: Argosy. 24-25: Alessia Girasole. 26: Alessia Girasole. 30: Deborah Melmon. 33: Deborah Melmon. 34-35: April Hartman

Photography Credits: All Photographs are by Macmillan/McGraw-hill (MMH) except as noted below.

1: Kevin Schafer/CORBIS. 2: (l) Burgess Blevins/Getty Images; (r) Alamy Images. 3: (b) Thinkstock/PunchStock; (t) Alaska Stock. 5: (bc) Mark Segal/Getty Images. 6: (bl) Danita Delimont/Alamy Images. 7: (br) Jim Baron/Image Finders. 9: (b) Mark Segal/Getty Images. 10: Lester Lefkowitz/Getty Images. 11: (l) David R. Frazier PhotoLibrary; (r) David R. Frazier PhotoLibrary. 13: Lester Lefkowitz/Getty Images. 14: Kevin Anthony Horgan/Getty Images. 15: SUNNYphotography.com/Alamy Images. 16: (b) Jake Rajs/Getty Images; (t) David Muench/CORBIS. 17: (b) Prisma/SuperStock; (t) Robert Glusic/Getty Images. 18: (c) Michael Melford/Getty Images. 18-19: (b) Jean-Pierre Pieuchot/Getty Images. 19: (c) Prisma/SuperStock; (t) Layne Kennedy/CORBIS. 20: Michelle D. Bridwell/PhotoEdit. 22: Alaska Stock. 23: Ariel Skelley/Blend Images/Jupiterimages. 25: (b) Stouffer Productions/Animals Animals. 27: (b) Ariel Skelley/Blend Images/Jupiterimages. 27: (t) Ariel Skelley/Getty Images. 28: (bc) Photowood Inc./Alamy Images; (bl) Ken Karp for MMH; (br) Ken Karp for MMH. 29: (bkgd) Photowood Inc./Alamy Images; (c) Ken Karp for MMH. 33: (b) National Aeronautics and Space Administration. 37: (b) Michelle D. Bridwell/PhotoEdit. 38: (b) Macmillan McGraw-Hill; (t) C Squared Studios/Getty Images. R1: (t) Mark Segal/Getty Images. R2: (bc) Layne Kennedy/CORBIS; (c) Robert Glusic/Getty Images; (tc) Michelle D. Bridwell/PhotoEdit. R3: (b) Ariel Skelley/Getty Images; (bc) Jake Rajs/Getty Images; (c) Jean-Pierre Pieuchot/Getty Images; (t) David Muench/CORBIS. R4: (bc) Jim Baron/Image Finders; (t) Michael Melford/Getty Images.